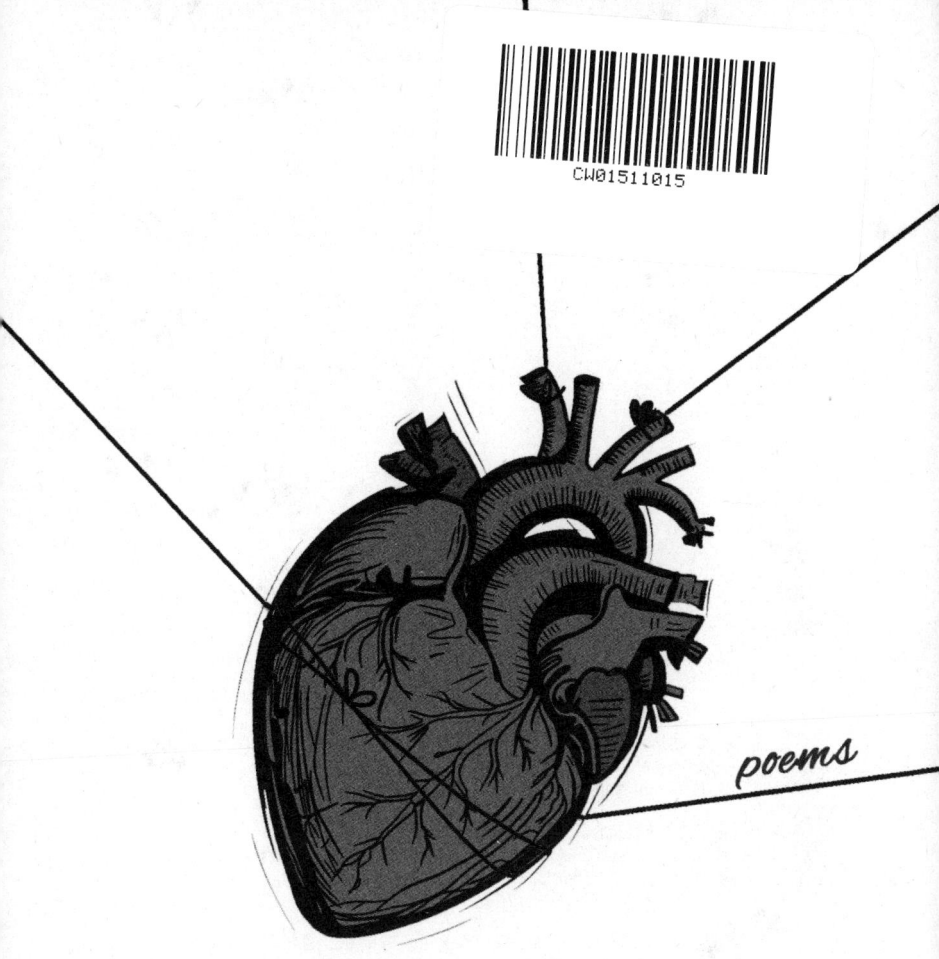

poems

lovers · exes · soulmates

elison alcovendaz

central
avenue
2025

Copyright © 2025 Elison Alcovendaz
Internal Design © 2025 Central Avenue Marketing Ltd.
Cover Design: © 2025 Becca Smallcombe

This is a work of fiction. Names, characters, places and incidents either are the
product of the author's imagination or are used fictitiously and any resemblance to
actual persons, living or dead, business establishments, events or locales is entirely
coincidental.

Published by Central Avenue Poetry, an imprint of Central Avenue Marketing Ltd.
www.centralavenuepublishing.com

LOVERS EXES SOULMATES: Poems

Trade Paperback: 978-1-77168-410-1
Ebook: 978-1-77168-411-8

Published in Canada
Printed in United States of America

1. POETRY / Asian American   2. POETRY / Love

1 3 5 7 9 10 8 6 4 2

for Patty

CONTENTS

LOVERS

SELF LOVE

SOULMATES

LOVERS

VIOLETS ARE VIOLET

Roses are red,
violets are blue—
wait. Aren't violets, violet?
I don't want to lie to you.
Roses are red,
violets are not blue.
Ugh! Still sounds cliché,
and you deserve something new.
Okay. Here goes.
Roses are thorny,
and being with you makes me . . .
no, no, can't say that.
Even though it's true,
it's way too corny.
Roses . . .
Roses are . . .
Roses are alright,
whether red or yellow or white
and some metaphor about light
and . . . and . . .
Dammit!
I just like you, okay?
I like you.
And I think we could be . . . something.
Maybe.
Wanna get tacos?

STORYTIME

If every person
is a book,
and I judged you
by your cover,
of course I'd say
you're beautiful
(because you are),
but more than that,
I'd want to know
your every word,
every page,
every chapter,
all the backstory,
the plot and all the subplots,
the voice,
the point of view,
the interior monologue,
the mood and
themes and
styles and
of course,
whether the protagonist
had room for me
in her story.

BOSS

If we were a video game,
you'd be the boss
at the end, and I'd need
100 lives
just to get to you.
But I wouldn't try to defeat you.
I'd just be happy to be there.
I'd lay down my weapons.
I'd tell you everything I endured
just to see you,
and you'd tell me those flames
you spewed were not
meant to kill, that you were
just protecting yourself.
Then I'd ask if you wanted to
end the game and go listen to music
or get cupcakes somewhere.
You'd say yes—

and we'd both win.

PARTS

Your knee
bumped my knee
and now,
for some reason,
all I can think about
is what it
might feel like
if the parts
of us
that are supposed
to touch,
touch.

KISS

A kiss is the beginning and ending of hunger.

A kiss is pleasure and pain.

A kiss is an agreement to create and destroy universes between lips, to break ourselves into a million greedy pieces until we have to glue ourselves back together again.

We kissed once, and I've spent every moment since trying to catch my breath.

THE PURPOSE OF A MOUTH

The mouth
is good
for four things:

1. eating
2. talking
3. kissing
4. breathing

So, tonight:

1. let's grab dinner
2. talk about how our days went
3. go home and kiss all the places on our bodies until
4. we're panting for breath

Or we can just skip to number 3?

BACKSEAT

We've got a backseat
kind of love,
a can't make it home in time
kind of love,
a pull over right here,
yes, right here,
yes, right now,
don't worry,
the windows will be so steamed
no one is going to see
(but they might hear)
kind of love.

READING

You're acting like a word,
when you're the whole story,
sitting hidden on the shelf,
when you deserve glory.
So dust yourself off,
and get ready to be read.
I'm coming to pick you up
and bring you back to bed.

SLOW LOVE

Speak slow.
When you say hello,
it should take days.
When you say my name,
it should take years.
When you say you love me,
entire civilizations should rise
and crumble into memory
before the words fall
from your mouth.
And in return,
I will teach you
the language of time,
when love and lust
were one movement,
when words were not meant
to be written or spoken,
but dreams to be pressed
into flesh by the heat
of divine hands.

REAL ESTATE

The next time I see you,
I'm going to wrap
my arms around you
and pull you in close,
as close as I can,
and introduce you
to your new home.

THREE LITTLE WORDS

I (Oh God am I really going to say this, what if she doesn't feel the same way, I don't want to scare her off, I don't want to pull open my chest just to hear her say she sees me as a friend, or maybe she'll just leave and never want to see me again, but I can't live in fear, right? I mean . . . I can't, right?) love (Yes, I can absolutely live in fear, it's perfectly fine to do that, oh no, what is that expression on her face, is that revulsion? A stomachache? Dammit, why did I even start saying this . . . oh yeah, it's because this is who I am, and it's okay to be who I am, and this could be the start of everything, but I could also just say anything else now . . . I love basketball . . . I love burritos . . . I love the way her lips curl when she's trying not to laugh at one of my stupid jokes . . .) you (I did it, I did it, I did it, I said it, but what is she doing now? Is she going to say it back? It doesn't matter, I'm proud of myself. I took the risk, and it doesn't matter now if she says it back but of course it matters because the entire universe is hanging in the balance here . . .)

DICTIONARY

Every person is a dictionary. Words mean different things to different people based on our unique experiences and memories.

This is why when I say, "I love you," I mean that I care about your happiness more than my own, that you are the first thing I think about in the morning and the last thing I think about at night, that there is an "us," that I see the mind and the heart of you, the end and the start of you, the whole and every part of you, that even if you are broken, I value every single piece.

But when I say, "I love you," you think I mean that I am going to hurt you, that you need to put your force field up because I'm just trying to get something from you, that I'm eventually going to find something unforgivably wrong about you, and so it'll just be easy to push me away so you can feel safe.

I want to keep reading you. So please stay and please keep reading me.

Even dictionaries can be revised.

HEARTSAFE

I'll pick open
the heartsafe you built.
I'll try with:
gentle hands,
strong hands,
sweet words,
sharp words,
and countless nights
of guessing combinations
of abracadabra things
I could do
or open sesame things
I could say.
If it turns out the key
is time—
to wait until you
feel loved enough by me
to open the safe yourself—
well, then I'll be here,
waiting.
Ready.

RAIN

If you feel like shrinking,
if you feel afraid,
I will be like the rain—
no matter how many coats you wear or
how many umbrellas you hold or
how small you make yourself—
I will be there until you let me in.

It might start with one drop
finding a space on the nape of your neck,
reminding you that you have a body,
a body meant to be touched,
a body meant to be held,
a body meant to be treasured,
until you raise your face to the sky,
umbrella down, coat off,
ready to let love in.

HOW I LOVE

Art is the act of making the unseen, seen.
(I will love you artfully)

Music is the act of making the unheard, heard.
(I will love you musically)

Poetry is the act of making the unsaid, said.
(I will love you poetically)

ALL YOU HAVE TO SAY

I will eat your music
and bathe in your voice
and heal your childhood
and drink your skin
and smoke your skeletons
and hug your memories
and dance in your lips
and sleep in your palms
and kiss your fractures
and burn your anxieties
and wear your breath
and kneel in your light
and sing your soul
and write poems in your scars.
You just have to say,
"I'm ready."

OCTOBER

I will love you like:

- the first sweater you put on in autumn
- warm apples
- blankets and books
- well-fitted boots and pumpkin patches
- crisp air and piles of leaves begging to be jumped in
- we're falling

But I will not forget to love you like we're
hanging on to summer, like no matter
how cool the world grows, there's always
room for heat, for wanting, for bare skin.

BREATH IMPLANTS

If the world ever becomes too much, or
if your life ever becomes too much,
and the millions of tiny, shallow breaths
never satisfy you, never fill you,
never allow you to overcome the fear
of your own dreams or the fear
of opening your heart because you feel
untethered, unsettled, unsafe—

I will offer you my breath.
I will offer it to you over and over again.

MESSY

We come to each other
        unclothed and
        unskinned,
just the bones of our ancestors and
the blood of past heartbreaks and
organs diseased from
        childhood grief and
        parental sins,
our nerves frayed from the pursuit
of decaying dreams.

We come to each other
a mess of
        bone blood disease nerves
and love each other
not in spite of it
but because of it.

THE SPACE

If someone were to ask me
how I know you're the one,
I would tell them:
there's a space
between my neck and shoulder
where only your head fits.

I WANTED TO WRITE AN ECLIPSE POEM

but there are already too many
metaphors about suns and moons.
So instead let me say,
I looked at your face one time,
and all I've seen
is light ever since.

THERE

In some remote part of the universe,
in a galaxy the shape of a square,
next to a moon the size of a penny,
on a planet the hue of your hair,
in a house the taste of a diamond,
in a book the length of a prayer,
a word exists to explain what we have,
not love, something more: there.

FLAVORS OF YOU

A forkful of rainbow
and a spoonful of tree,
a sliver of sunrise
and a warm cup of tea.

A slice of horizon
and a helping of dew,
a dollop of moonlight
and two scoops of blue.

A pinch of July heat,
and a shot glass of flame,
a bowlful of snowflakes
and a bottle of rain.

Add honey and beach
and clouds and soil, too;
the whole world exists
in the flavors of you.

CUPID

I did not get shot
with Cupid's
puny little arrow.
I got hit by
a comet—
an apocalyptic event
so devastating,
my only two
possibilities
were to die
or to love you.

THE BEST THING

Come rest right here, baby.
I'm not going anywhere.
I'll stay until a thousand suns go down,
running my fingers through your hair.
You don't have to say anything,
because I already know
the bruises no one else sees,
the scars you never show.
It's just you and me right now,
forget the world outside.
Let me kiss away the hurt.
Let me bring back to life what died.

And when that day comes,
I hope you'll understand,
you are the best thing, baby,
and I'm lucky to be your man.

BUCKETS

Something is broken inside of me.
No, I don't need you to repair it.
But the burden is getting heavy,
and I'd be willing to share it.

And in return, if there's pain
flooding inside of you,
let me know, and I'd be glad
to fill some of my buckets, too.

WALK WITH ME

Take a walk with me.
We'll stop in the shade and
dip our toes in the lake and
I hope you'll talk with me

about what's been ailing you.
I'll listen to every breath and
I'll listen to every word about
how the world has been failing you.

I can't promise answers,
but I can promise presence, and
I can promise to be here
no matter how the dark dances

and swirls through your mind.
You can scream.
You can cry.
Just don't say you're fine.

Walk with me.

RUN-ON

I won't love you like this.
Short. Declarative.

Or love you like this?
Too hesitant, unknowing.

Or love you like this!
Too showy, too loud.

(Or love you like this.)
Trivial, a second thought.

I will love you like a run-on, one that
never stops, one that keeps
finding ways to keep on going and
breaks the rules when it feels like
it because if love can be stopped
with a period or a question mark or
an exclamation point or even a
semicolon (even if used improperly);
then it isn't real love but rather what
someone else has told you is love,
and that can't be true for us, for our
love is unruly yet calm, wild yet still
makes sense, a whole library told in
a sentence that never stops . . .

IN UNREPORTED NEWS, THINGS HAPPENING AT THIS EXACT MOMENT

Two people are on a first date, sitting across from each other thinking, "This is the one!"

An alcoholic is taking their last drink before getting sober.

A mother is looking into her baby's eyes for the first time.

Someone is holding a door open.

Someone is saying "thank you."

A father is pushing a child on a swing.

A child is laughing.

I am loving you.

WHEN YOUR SCARS SPEAK

I will listen.
I know they do not yell.
I know they harmonize
in a thousand whispers,
luring you to lie down
in the dark-lit meadow
of yourself
where the grass grows long,
and the soil
knows your secrets.
I will stay beside you,
and when you wake,
I will be there with
my hand outstretched,
ready to help you up.

BLOWTORCH

We're always at our best
when we're putting out a fire,
so we set each other aflame
and mistake it for desire.

You're addicted to the heat.
I'm addicted to the smoke.
We're addicted to saving each other
when we start to choke.

You bring the gasoline.
I bring the matches.
Neither of us bring water
so we end up in ashes.

Maybe we should stop,
since arson is a crime.
Nah, grab the blowtorch,
and burn me one more time.

EXES

THE CLIFF

Hanging on the edge again—
how do we always end up here?
I'm trying to hold on,
but I know that we're
losing our grip
on everything that's real,
fingers slipping through
all the love we used to feel.

Hanging on the edge again;
here comes the final price.
Maybe we let go this time
or maybe we roll the dice
and pull ourselves back up
and promise to be true,
though sabotaging promises
for us is nothing new.

Hanging on the edge again,
a question of when, not if.
That's what happens when you love
so close to the cliff.

8:18

You said you'd be home by eight.
It's 8:18, and
I've already imagined
your car overturned on the highway or
you being abducted by aliens or
you happily in someone else's arms or
even worse,
you sitting somewhere alone—
a sticky restaurant booth,
a dark parking lot,
a smoky bar—
alone,
choosing to be alone,
because even that would be better
than returning to me.

THE MEDICINE CABINET

- Anti-fever pills for those late nights with you
- An inhaler for my lungs whenever you look at me
- Pain relievers for every time you leave
- Heartburn meds for the words I have to swallow
- Sleep aids for the nights you don't come home
- Skin cream for the places you leave untouched
- Anti-nausea pills for all the trips I took to close the distance between us
- Eye drops to help me see in the darkness
- Anti-anxiety meds for the person I've become loving you

THIS

You said you couldn't do *this* anymore,
and that's what hit me the most—
not your "it's not you, it's me" lies and
not your "I wish things were different" lies—
no,
it was your use of "this,"
a no-name,
almost nothing,
barely even a word
word
to describe what
I thought had been
everything.

THE MOVIE OF MY LIFE

You are a memory of a memory,
a background actor in the movie of my life,
and yet your face demands the camera,
and your presence demands attention,
so now I am worried the film about my life
has become the story about how I will never
get over you.

THE SPEED OF LOSS

They say nothing
is faster than the
speed of light,
but when you left,
how swift the darkness came.
And then I wonder:
have scientists
ever been in love?
Then they'd know
the only thing faster
than the speed of light
is the loss of it.

IF I COULD, I WOULD

If I could, I would
reset the game,
die a hundred times
to forget your name,
because you hurt me (bad)
and I'm still hurting (sad).

If I could, I would
live in outer space,
build a home on Mars
to forget your face,
because you hurt me (bad)
and I'm still hurting (sad).

But here I am lying to myself again,
trying to keep the pain small.
Being hurt by you is better than
feeling nothing at all.

LUCID DREAMING

I read online that some people
can learn to control their dreams,
but I've tried for years, and
I still haven't won the lottery,
I still haven't written a bestseller,
I still don't look like Thor,
cupcakes still aren't healthy,
and you're still somewhere else,
not loving me.

ALL THE THINGS

Can you please just come back I'm tired and I'm lonely and my head is pounding and I just I just I just need you like right here like right next to me so I can rest my head I just really need to rest my head on something familiar on someone familiar on someone who loves me or at least used to love me someone please I'm so tired and I'm tasting colors but nothing too colorful just the pale green of your eyes and the pale pink of your lips and I don't know what to do you used to help me know what to do but I'm tired and hungry and I should eat something but there's nothing in the fridge except all the things I should've said when you were right next to me I wish you were next to me.

ARE YOU AWAKE?

I know I shouldn't be texting you,
especially at 1 a.m.,
but I'm not texting you for *that* reason,
but because
you always say the funniest things,
and I've been up
all night,
just running through my thoughts,
stumbling in the dark
for many consecutive 1 a.m.'s now,
and I know it's not your responsibility,
but
I could really use a laugh,
I could really use some light, and
the only person I could think of
who brought both to my life
was you.

ASH

Maybe we were just lovedrunk idiots with invincible hearts who spoke carelessly of forever. Something in me has changed now. I'm uncertain about everything. We were so confident. We etched our initials into old tree trunks as though the world were a permanent thing for us to imprint our love upon, as though there would never be a day when we'd be chopped into pieces and thrown into a fire, and yet here I am, burning.

NO OTHER HEARTS WERE HARMED IN THE FILMING OF THIS LIFE

Just mine,
over
and
over
and
over again

(but I guess that means it heals over and over and over again, too).

SCAR OF YOU

The biggest scar I have
is the one no one can see.
It starts inside my brain
and runs through all of me.
When it scabs, I pick it,
to let the fresh blood spring.
When it floods my body,
I remember everything.
The doctor thinks I'm broken,
and I need to let things heal.
He doesn't understand the scar
of you is the only thing I feel.

DÉJÀ VU

I missed holding you,
so I held a cactus,
but that didn't quite feel like you,
so I held some broken glass,
but that still wasn't quite right,
so I held the blade of a knife
as tightly as I could,
and when the blood
really started to gush,
and a puddle formed on the ground,
I thought: "That's more like it."

UNSPOKEN

I cannot speak your name
for fear of losing you again,
so I keep you
inside my lips,
letting you flavor
every breath
I inhale and
every breath
I give back to the world,
so everyone knows
(or at least I know)
you're not gone,
you're still here,
you're still with me.

ICE CREAM

We hadn't seen each other in so long, so when you asked me how I'd been, instead of telling you about the new diagnosis and the new meds and the new job and the old self-doubt, I thought about how we used to make late night runs to the gas station for ice cream, and how you would always finish before me, and how I would always let you have the rest of mine because even though ice cream had been my most favorite thing in the world, it could not compete with the way your lips moved, or how your eyes deepened when the sugar hit your tongue, or the way the chocolate lingered in your mouth, and that's why I didn't respond at the time, because I was too busy tasting our past.

DECAPITATION

I'm falling apart slowly.

First, the fingertips fall. The fingertips that ran slow marathons up and down your neck, the fingertips that knew all the ticklish spots on your body, the fingertips that typed you thousands upon thousands of texts just to say I was thinking of you.

Second, the hands. The hands that cupped your face and wiped the floods from your eyes, the hands that held yours like they were the final piece to the puzzle, the hands that regret waving goodbye.

Then, the arms. The arms that held you when the entire world felt like monsters from your childhood, the arms that swam and swam after you when you floated too far away.

Next, the lips. The lips that never told you a lie (except that one time I told you I hated you), the lips that made a home of every spot on your body, the lips that shouted my love for you to the world, the lips still trembling from the ghost of your kiss.

Then, the ears. The ears that could tie an emotion to every shade of your voice, the ears that still hear your breath in every moment the universe moves.

Next, the head. The head that bobbed in rhythm whenever you broke out in song, the head that seemed to find itself on your pillow every night (I'm sorry about that), the head that still wears the 49ers hat you bought me years ago for my birthday.

Soon after, the torso falls. The torso you rested your head on when the days turned gray, the torso still trying to find its heartbeat.

Last, the legs. The legs that ran to you but never from you, the legs that, someday, will pick themselves back up and take a few tentative steps into this without-you-world and find a way to piece myself back together.

HERE, THERE, EVERYWHERE

Here
I am
Somewhere else
you are
Nowhere
is love
Everywhere
is pain

MOVING

The town reminded me of you,
so I moved to another city,
but the energy reminded me of you,
so I moved to another state,
but the rain reminded me of you,
so I moved to another country,
but the art reminded me of you,
so I moved to Venus,
but the heat reminded me of you,
so I moved to Saturn,
but the cold reminded me of you,
so I moved to another galaxy,
but the stars reminded me of you,
so I moved to a black hole,
and the nothingness reminded me of you
more than anything else had ever reminded me of you
and so I stayed there.

A MILLION DREAMS

Every teardrop is a dream,
and I have cried
a million dreams.
Some small (your hair on my pillow),
some large (the touch of your hand),
and yet the dreams
never leave me.

They fall halfway down my cheeks
and dissolve back into my skin,
a million dreams

(your skin   your lips   your voice
          your mind   your heart   your love)

cried and re-absorbed
back into me
over and over again.

BRUISED

Sometimes I'll find a bruise on my body
and spend too much time
trying to figure out where it came from
only to realize it's the memory of you
still holding on.

YOU'VE REACHED THE VOICE MAIL TO MY HEART

But first of all, how did you even get this number?

I guess it doesn't matter.

Go ahead and leave whatever message you're going to leave.

Just make it quick.

Or don't.

I mean, if you want to leave a longer message, it might . . .

It might be nice to hear someone's voice.

Whoever you are.

Thanks for calling.

Seriously, it means a lot.

It's not like people are actually intending to reach me nowadays.

Lots of telemarketers.

Sometimes I stay on the phone with them just to talk to someone.

Sorry, I'm rambling.

I don't even know if I know you.

Do you know me?

I guess you must, unless it's a wrong number.

Or you're trying to sell me a car warranty.

In any case, just leave a message after the beep.

I'll return your call.

I hope you'll answer.

REINCARNATION

When asked what I wanted to be reincarnated as, I said I wanted to be the spider that crawls onto your face in the middle of the night and bites your mouth. That way I can make you feel some of the pain you made me feel while touching your lips again.

THINGS MY EX AND DOCTOR HAVE BOTH SAID

Breathe
You need to do something about your stress
Breathe
Does it hurt when I press here?
You should talk to someone
Deep breath this time
There might be something wrong with your heart
I can't make the changes for you
Remember to breathe
I hope you're better the next time I see you
Take care of yourself

AUCTION

When they auctioned my body parts, I didn't think you'd come, but you did. They saved my heart for last. You stood in the back of the room, quietly raising your hand as the price soared:

- $5,000
- $20,000
- $50,000

When you won, I thought you had done so to reclaim the small part of you that still had a home inside me, but when you won with a bid of $100,000, you claimed your winnings, drove to the coast, and threw my heart into the Pacific.

THE SKIN STORE

After you left, I went to The Skin Store. I stayed there all day, trying on all the skins: tighter, looser, lighter, darker, older, younger, smoother, rougher, thinner, thicker, but nothing felt right.

"Any of these work for you?" the saleswoman asked.

I shook my head.

"I'm so sorry," she said. "We've never had a dissatisfied customer. What are you looking for?"

I told her that I needed to forget you, to forget the way you touched me, the way you rested your hand on the inside of my thigh at football games, the way you kissed that one spot on the back of my neck, the way you pressed your forehead to my forehead when the anxious thoughts came, but no matter how many skins I tried on, I couldn't forget you, as though your fingerprints and lips had imprinted inside me, as if you had infiltrated me, invaded my bones, and injected my marrow with the disease of your vanished love.

"Oh, honey," she said, nodding knowingly, "you might want to try The Heart Store instead."

THE HEART STORE

"I have never seen this level of broken-heartedness," the worker said.

"So you can't help?" I asked.

"You've tried every heart we have here. I'm really sorry."

"So where do I go?"

"There's nowhere to go," the worker said. "There's only time."

THE MUSEUM OF US

The most popular exhibit in The Museum of Us is the caricature we had made that day at Fisherman's Wharf. Do you remember?

You were so happy. At least I thought you were.

But now, when people see the caricature, they speak quietly about the lightlessness in your face, the swirly galaxy of hurt in your eyes. But all I remember is the chowder on your breath, the salty air pressing your clothes against you.

I didn't know it was already over.

I walk from exhibit to exhibit, looking at our memories on display, listening to strangers whisper about your pain. Why can the world see in your face what I never could?

I didn't see you. I never did.

There are countless wings and rooms and whole floors dedicated to other relationships. But the curator tells me ours is the most popular. She says people line up for hours in advance to be the first in the room. She says people cry here. She says couples come here to find answers. She says that finally, people see you.

COUCH

I found memory in the crevices of the couch. The cookie crumbs that fell from your lips because you were laughing too hard. The coin we used to flip when we couldn't decide what to watch. The scrunchie that slid off your hair one of those nights we couldn't make it to the bedroom. The Kleenex you used when your grandpa died.

I know I should sell this couch. Or donate it, maybe. But it's not mine. It's ours. It's something we bought together. And these aren't sad memories anymore. They remind me that, at one time, I was worthy enough to be loved by someone like you. And I will be again.

THE CALENDAR SAYS IT'S TIME FOR A HAPPY POEM

but for some reason you stopped blocking me on Instagram, and I've spent the last two days sleeplessly scrolling through all the photos you've posted since we ended, and I've never seen your smile so . . . smiley, as if you really mean it and aren't just posing for pictures, and now I'm wondering if you're just doing this to fuck with me, knowing I'd be unable to stay away, even if it's just social media, or perhaps you're telling me the truth, that the reason you never smiled this way when we were together was that I couldn't make you happy, and then I realize maybe there is a happy poem in there somewhere, something about my heartache being the gateway to you finding joy, and so I guess it's time to unfriend you once and for all . . .

BEST VERSION

I saw you at Starbucks,
and I think you saw me, too.
I knew I looked a mess,
while you looked something new.
You ordered a different drink,
something something skinny.
I wanted to maybe pay for it,
but I didn't have it in me.
You were happy and gleaming.
You were a star out of reach.
And in that moment, I learned
what years could never teach.
I wanted the best version of you,
but now I truly see,
the best version of you
is the one without me.

HOW TO LOVE

Breathe. Cry. See. Laugh. Hear.
Fight. Give. Doubt. Leave. Burn.
Run. Drink. Dance. Bloom. Fall.
Fly. Climb. Grieve. Speak. Play.
Work. Fuck. Swim. Break. Kneel.
Sin. Smell. Bleed. Sigh. Jump.
Stay. Touch. Search. Fear. Taste.
Drown. Swim. Sing. Build. Feed.
Change. Shout. Bare. Rise. Swell.
Sweat. Kiss. Feel. Act. Dare.
Shine. Run. Purge. Want. Dream.
Dive. Think. Try. Lose. Heal.

Grow.

SELF-LOVE
(An Interlude)

BROKEN

Dear Self,

You know there's no such thing as a broken heart, right?

"Broken" means not working.

"Broken" means malfunctioning.

But when you're feeling sad, lonely, frustrated, angry, helpless—
"broken hearted"—your heart is actually functioning the way it's
supposed to. It's making you feel. It's making you grow. It's making you
learn. It's making you heal.

A beating heart is never broken, and because it isn't broken, it will do
what it always does. It will love, and be loved, again.

Love,
Self

WORTHY. EVERYTHING.

If you cannot know
light without dark or
joy without sorrow,
then can you know who you are
without first knowing
who you are not?

You are not
your libraries of mistakes or
your playlists of regretful words or
your calendars of weak moments or
your closets of heartbreak and sins or
the times you thought
you were too good for someone or
the times you thought
you were not good enough for anyone.

You are not unworthy.
You are not nothing.
You are . . .

BE A CHILD

There are only two things you need to know to overcome heartbreak.

You learned the first thing when you were born: breathe.

You learned the second thing before you were two years old: take a step forward.

Be a child. Breathe. Take a step forward. Again. And again. And again.

NEW SONG

If you close your eyes and listen,
you'll hear a concert inside yourself,
a chorus of your past selves,
each bringing a different sound,
creating a cacophony
of pain and sorrow.
They sing the old songs
with all the wrong instruments and
all the wrong notes and
all the wrong lyrics,
and yet, as you listen,
you hear something new,
something beautiful and complete,
something that would not have existed
without all of that heartbreak.
Once a note is sung and played, it is gone.
Let it stay there.
Instead, grab the mic and
sing a new song.
A song of self-acceptance.
Sing you.

GREENHOUSE

Mind where you plant your time;
your garden marks your home.
If you spread roots in toxic ground,
your seeds will not be sown.

You will not find every nutrient
in the earth of someone else,
you will often need to find
water, soil, and sun within yourself.

When the world sees your color,
they'll come to catch a view,
and you can tell them to get lost
or bring one close to the new you.

Growth attracts growth,
bloom fertilizes bloom,
tending to your own greenhouse
brings other light into the room.

THE NATURE OF THINGS

Look at that scar,
the way it raises above your skin,
occupying more space
than it did before.

This is the nature of wounds.
This is the nature of breaking.
This is the nature of living.

For how could we become
the best version of ourselves
if our bodies and hearts
did not open from time to time
to create more room
for love and hope to grow?

THE PERSON OF YOUR DREAMS

Imagine you found the person of your dreams. Imagine all the things you'd say to them. How beautiful they are. How smart they are. How funny. How generous. How creative. How much you just want to spend time with them, to be in their company, to be in their glow. How despite their weaknesses and flaws, you could not imagine loving anyone or anything more.

Now say the same things to the mirror.

LUCKY PENNY

You drop a penny, and it becomes someone's lucky penny.

You plant a rosebush in your front yard, and those colors are the only thing that entices your elderly neighbors to get out for a walk.

You see litter on the ground, and you pick it up and place it in the trash, giving the janitor just enough time to get home and kiss his kids goodnight.

You make eye contact with a stranger, and it's the first time they've felt seen since forever.

You post something—a poem, a song, a quote—and it saves someone's life.

When you open yourself to give love to the world, the world gives it back to you.

We're all someone's lucky penny, and a single cent can go a long way.

INFINITE LIBRARY

The entrance to the Infinite Library was in a cloud on top of a mountain. It had taken me decades to find it. The floor seemed to be made of glass, for I could see the universe swirling below my feet as I strode among the endless shelves and floors of books on every subject imaginable—tarot, micropoetry, even the mating rituals of unicorns.

I roamed from section to section, searching for any book that could teach me how to get you back. After years of futility, a librarian in a white dress approached and asked what I needed, so I told her.

"Ah," she said. "So you need the section on love." She pointed to the pathway behind me. "Walk in that direction and you will find it."

"How far?" I asked.

"You'll see," she said.

And so I walked. And walked. I walked past countless sections on Self-Help, others on Self-Improvement, yet others on Communication Skills. Before I knew it, my hair started to go gray, my back hurt, and my vision grew blurry. Still, I kept walking until finally, I fell.

"Hello again."

I sat up to find the librarian in her white dress standing before me.

"How much further?" I asked.

"That depends," she said.

"On what?"

"On you."

"Look, I don't know what kind of game you're playing here," I said, getting to my feet, "but I don't have much time left and I need to get her back. Please."

She looked upon me with a soft smile on her face.

"And yet," she said, "you walked past every section that could've helped you."

"What the hell are you talking about? You said I needed the section on love, you said I needed to walk in this direction!"

"There is no section on love," she said. "There is no instruction manual. There is no magical formula. The only thing you can do is to try and better yourself, to love yourself, and when you do that, when you try to be your best, you give yourself the opportunity for your soulmate to find you."

"Soulmate?" I asked. "You say that as if it's not *her*."

"We must earn our soulmates. Love has a lot of lessons to teach us. Some learn faster than others. Some never learn at all. This *her* you speak of. Perhaps she is the lesson. Perhaps she is what you needed to become worthy of your true soulmate."

"How will I know who she is?"

"You do as I suggest, and you will know. The knowing is the easy part."

The librarian disappeared behind a wall of mist, and the next thing I knew, I was back in my bed, staring at the sunrise through my window, knowing that finally, I knew what I had to do and who I had to be.

SOULMATES

THE CREATION OF LANGUAGE

If we did not have language,
I would create the word "light"
from the fire in your eyes
and the word "home"
from the warmth of your thighs
and the word "strength"
from the jut of your chin
and the word "taste"
from the sweet salt of your skin.

I would create the word "water"
from the wet of your lips
and the word "dance"
from the curve of your hips
and the word "time"
from the scars on your wrists
and the word "survive"
from the strength of your fists.

But I would not create a word for "love."
We would live that, instead.

THEY WILL REMEMBER

When there are no more metaphors
and poetry ceases to exist,
when hands are no longer held,
and lips no longer kissed . . .

When songs remain unsung,
and guitars sit unplayed,
when hips stay untouched,
and beds stay made . . .

When seeds never bloom,
and the sun fails to rise,
when wishes stay unspoken,
and stars abandon the skies . . .

the world will see us and remember.

They will remember music.
They will remember dreams.
They will remember desire.
They will remember love.

WHAT THE UNIVERSE WANTS

Each word is jealous of another word.
A car yearns to be a plane.
A plane yearns to be a rocket.
A rocket yearns to be a star.
A star yearns to be a galaxy.
A galaxy yearns to be a universe.
Every word yearns to be more—except love.
Love is happy with itself.
Love is the means.
Love is the end.
So when I say I love you,
I say I desire nothing more.
Loving you and being loved by you
is what the universe yearns to be.

THE NATURE OF A SENTENCE

A sentence, by its nature, can rarely be received the way it's intended. Every word curves and bends its meaning to our own lives and experiences.

This is why when I say I love you, you think I'm talking about a dream, an improbability, because everyone who has said that to you has hurt you or left you or both, but when I say I love you, I'm talking about what is, right now, the gritty light of our lives, the roses growing from the cracks, the cathartic eulogy to our youthful bodies, the joyful and monotonous rhythm of being lovers for only a few moments in the day when we are not being parents or bosses or coworkers or siblings or children, the invisible yet connected stretch marks that tell us our hearts have grown larger and closer together.

A sentence, by its nature, can rarely be received the way it's intended. Sometimes, you need more words to make your meaning plain. In other words, I love you.

THE FIRST SUNRISE

Imagine the first time
the first human saw
their first sunrise,
now imagine
the immense joy
and amazement
and warmth
they must've felt,
now understand
that is absolutely nothing
compared to how I feel
waking up every morning,
and the first thing
I see is your face.

THE ONE

Despite the title of this poem,
finding "The One" does not
guarantee a happily ever after.
This isn't a fairy tale
or a Disney movie.
But there are choices, and
the most loving thing
anyone can do is to choose
that person,
every morning,
every hour,
every minute,
every moment.
So here on our
wedding day
and all the moments
to come,
I choose you.

THE BEGINNING AND THE END

Somewhere in the universe, there is a beginning. A beginning without end. A beginning with infinite momentum.

Civilizations throughout space and time, human and alien, will seek understanding. Their most brilliant minds will dedicate their entire lives to discovering the nature of this beginning—where it started, how it started, why it never ends.

All of them will fail.

What they'll never understand is that everything begins and ends with two human beings loving each other more than any other living thing has loved another living thing.

You and me.

Then. Now. Forever.

BINGE

When there's nothing on Netflix
and no books on your shelves
and no songs on your playlists,

I'll kiss you a film.
I'll touch you a novel.
I'll love you a song.

WHY

Amazon knows what books I like,
Facebook my political party of choice.
Google knows the places I've been,
Apple the sound of my voice.
Technology knows the What of me.
It knows the Where, How, and When.
Its brain is working constantly
on algorithms and trends.
But it'll never get to the Why of me,
that it'll never be able to do.
Because it would need a heart to see
the Why of me is you.

FOREVER

Someone once told me:

People lose their soulmates all the time.

Why? I asked.

They get lazy.

I don't understand.

They think it'll just magically "work." They let things get in the way. Kids. Money. Jealousy. Could be anything.

So what do I do?

You remember that all relationships take effort, and the one you have with your soulmate is worth the most effort. You must try. You must keep trying. Blood. Sweat. Tears. Conversations. Dates. Hugs. Kisses. All of it. Keep trying.

Okay.

Forever doesn't happen by itself.

PLAYLIST

We made a playlist.

The first song is the sound of the alarm clock. Then the hum of running water. The baby crying. The pop of the toaster. The jingle of keys. The rumble of the car. The clack of fingers to keyboards. The dings of text messages. The drone of coworkers talking. The honks of vehicles in traffic. The sizzle of dinner on the pan. The intro song to whatever TV show we're watching. The rustle of the toothbrush. The squeak of the bed. The goodnight kiss. Silence.

We made a playlist, and it's killing us.

HONEYMOON

We stood on the beach, hand in hand,
the warm ocean sifting sand beneath our feet.
We stared at the horizon, leaning into each other,
the Hawaiian sun glinting off our wedding rings,
the endless hope of the future before us.

What were you dreaming of then?
Certainly, it was not this—
currents of monotony
eroding the sandcastle we built,
little by little,
while all we do is stand by,
just watching it disappear.

MESSAGE IN A BOTTLE

There's an ocean between us,
and I never learned to swim.
Every time I try, I drown,
death whispering its hymn.

I once even got on a boat,
despite my fear of water.
But the storms left me shipwrecked
in wet and wooden slaughter.

And then I wonder why
you look so cozy on the shore,
sipping your piña colada
while I keep trying to find more

ways to traverse
the foreboding, silent sea.
And yet you've never once tried
to find your way back to me.

Instead of swimming or sailing,
I'll try something else instead.
I'll put this message in a bottle
and slide it across the bed.

THE OLD LANGUAGE

We spent years speaking
a language only the two of us knew,
a language that took time to speak,
a language that used mouths and hands,
but the world and all its quickness got to us,
and now we sit on the same couch
or lay in the same bed
texting soulless words to each other,
but never spend the night
rolling around in bed
with love in our hearts
and lust on our lips.

THE BIGGEST MISTAKE OF MY LIFE

It was 8 p.m. when I heard the knock on the door. You were sleeping on the couch. I got up quietly and answered the door.

It was me, but an older me. Still tall, but leaning on a wooden cane, hunched forward as though exhaling would knock him over.

"Hi," he said.

His voice was hushed and raspy, his face forlorn. He stared at me with eyes that longed to be looked into, as though no one had looked at him with loving eyes in a very long time.

"What are you doing here?" I asked.

"Preventing you from making the biggest mistake of your life," he said. "If my calculations are correct, you're planning on asking for a trial separation tomorrow."

"Yeah," I said, eyes locked to the ground.

"Don't," he said. "It's up to you to rise to her. Do better. Be better."

"But—"

He slapped me with his cane.

"No buts," he said. "I've spent the last forty years of my life conquering time travel *just for this moment*. When you find your home in someone's love, that's the best there ever is. There is nothing better, no matter what might be going through your head right now. Do you understand?"

I nodded.

He leaned sideways and saw you sleeping on the couch. He looked only for a moment before his eyes began dripping, his shaky hand clutched to his chest.

"There is nothing now, in the past or in the future, as beautiful as her."

A few moments passed before he slid up his sleeve and pushed a button on his watch.

"Be worthy of her," he said just before he disappeared.

"What are you doing?"

I spun around to find you standing a few feet away, wearing a wrinkled t-shirt and baggy pajama pants, hair a mess, rubbing your eyes. I ran to you and kissed you as true and full as I could.

"Just remembering what it's like to be the luckiest man in the world," I said.

I'M TRYING (PART 1)

You loved me
at my worst,
so you deserve
to be loved
by my best.

MAY I?

I fell in love with the way you danced—
carefree, wild—
but now when I play our song,
you roll your eyes.
Was it really that long ago?
Take my hand.
Stand.
Spin with me.
We killed the music,
but that means we can
revive it, too.

UNPLUGGED

Let's go out into the world alone
and leave our phones at home
and run our fingers across the sky.

Let's ignore the texts and alerts
and just put each other first.
Everyone else gets no reply.

Let's reacquaint our touch
in ways slow and sure, no rush,
and look into each other, eye to eye.

Let's remind ourselves of us
and how we fell in love and lust
and how we could get each other high.

US

What is love but a constant choosing?
Now. Now. Now again.
There is nothing keeping us here.
No guns to our heads.
No gods.
Just waking up each day and knowing
we could make a million different choices
and yet we choose the same thing
over and over and over again.

Us.

CARDS

I bought you a birthday card
and an anniversary card
and a Valentine's Day card
and a Mother's Day card
and a Christmas card
and a few just because cards,
but none of them said
what I wanted to say,
so I started writing poems,
and I haven't stopped yet,
and I don't think I'll finish
before I'm dead,
but I intend to spend
the rest of my life
showing you
what I want to say,
so even if you never read
the poems I've written,
you'll know
how home you are to me,
anyway.

THE VIEW

If you look out the same window
at different times on different days,
you'll see:

> *the sky turn blue to orange to gray*
> *leaves fall and leaves grow*
> *streetlights shine and dim*
> *roads fill and empty as*
> *sun to rain to snow to sun*
> *casts the world in the eternal cycle*
> *of light to dark to light*

and yet the view hasn't changed at all—
only your perception.

After many years with you,
our bodies have grown heavy to light to heavy, and
our faces have earned the wrinkles of experience,
gaining smiles and losing them and rediscovering them, but as

> *the roads are the same roads*
> *the streetlights the same streetlights*
> *the trees the same trees*
> *the sky the same sky*

so too is your body and your face and your soul.

Beauty is still beauty.
Love is still love.

And I will never get tired of the view.

WRINKLED

We held hands, exchanged rings,
you carried something blue . . .

We had kids, bought a house,
accomplished a thing or two . . .

We got sad, we had fights,
but somehow made it through . . .

We lost love, recreated love,
found a way to make it new . . .

Now all that's left is the thing
I always vowed to do . . .

To share a life, and walk slow,
and get wrinkled with you.

LIGHTNING AND THUNDER

When we first met, seeing you
was like tasting lightning. And
though years have passed, and
you have grown more concerned
about your wrinkles, your
weight, the way time has changed
your body, I want you to know
that when I see you, I still
taste thunderstorms.

CO-AUTHOR

Time tells the stories.

Time tells how many times we have to say "I am enough" before we believe it.

Time tells whether we get our fingers around the dreams we're chasing.

Time tells whether we get the girl or the boy or the job or the scholarship.

Or the disease.

Time tells whether we ever become the protagonist in our own story.

Time tells of the breaths and the deaths and everything in between.

The loves. The losses. The lessons.

Time tells the stories.

But time doesn't write them.

We do.

And the story we've co-authored . . .

Well, it's the best that's ever been told.

UNFINISHED

If you died tomorrow,
you'd still live forever
in my Notes app—
a never-ending list of
unfinished poems
that will
never be right and
never be perfect
and yet,
I will edit them
until my last breath
trying to make them
worthy of you.

I'M TRYING (PART 2)

When they said you were gone, I thought that was impossible—I'd just kissed you, I'd just told you a joke you pity-laughed at—so I ran to show the doctors how alive you were, but you wore an expression that I'd never seen before, completely free of demons, and so now I'm here, hugging you, well not you, but the body that used to contain you because you, you are somewhere else, somewhere far, far away, like Neverland or the North Pole or on a spaceship flying at the speed of light away from me, from us, from the life we built with our scarred, fractured hands, and I'm trying, you hear me, I'm trying to bring you back, but I see that softness in your face again, and I know you're already floating, you're already out the window, you're already in the sky, carrying my heart with you.

LOVE POEM

A poem is just a poem
until your soulmate dies,
and their last breaths
are the cadence for the rhymes,
and their last words
are inspiration for the lines,
and your face is
the last stanza in their eyes.

A poem is just a poem
until you realize,
we're born into silence
but find verse among the cries,
we're born into death
but find life among the trials,
and we're more than metaphor,
for a poem never dies.

A BETTER PLACE

They said you're in a better place,
but I don't understand.
What better place could there be
than here, holding my hand?
They said you're in a better place,
where pain can never start,
but is it really a better place
if you no longer have your heart?
They said you're in a better place
filled with endless light,
but how could a place be better
without us snuggling at night?
They said you're in a better place
where you're at peace and free,
but how could it be a better place
if you're so far away from me?
They said you're in a better place.
I'll have to hope that's true.
I've never been in a worse place.
I guess waiting will have to do.

THE LAST GOODBYE BEFORE THE ETERNAL HELLO

Everyone is wearing their finest clothes.
Everyone has gathered the most colorful flowers.
Everyone is shedding their heaviest tears.
Everyone is sharing their funniest memories.
Everyone is sending you all the words they didn't say.

Let us say goodbye for the last time.

When we meet again, we will greet each other with the eternal hello.

WEIGHTLESS

I never saw the invisible planets that I carried on my shoulders after you passed. I only felt them. Little by little, day by day, growing heavier, pushing me closer and closer to the floor.

And then it happened.

A crumpling. A crumbling.

Not one more moment of effort to give.

I lay on the cold floor. Eyes closed. Barely breathing. I thought about your face the first time I saw you, the depth of your eyes, and the immediate pull of that cosmic rope inside me, that rope that ended inside you. I thought about the life we made together, the nights we laughed until our sides cramped, the tears we wiped from each other's eyes, every kiss, every fight, every moment building like a ladder up to the sky.

When I finally opened my eyes and saw you standing there with your arm outstretched, a perfect smile on your perfect face, the mountains of fear and continents of grief and oceans of loneliness rolled off me.

You helped me up and we walked, together, towards the light.

ON MY WAY

If someone needs to find me,
I'll be flying high,
wearing cool cloudskin
with stardrops in my eyes.

I'm on a journey
to the boundary of space,
catching cosmic glitter
in the crevices of my face.

I'm told that's where you live now,
beyond the reach of light,
and darkness has engulfed you
in mute, enduring night.

I promise I will find you
and build a home nearby
and take the sun out of my chest
and pin it to the sky.

SKYLAND

The sky is a neighborhood, and
I've saved some acreage for you.
Cloudless and unblemished,
a perfect patch of blue.
I've been waiting impatiently,
but you had your life to lead,
until the day came
for your soul to be freed.
Let me escort you to our forever;
we can do anything with our land.
Grow a meadow, create a mountain,
build a real castle in the sand.
Once you settle in,
and peace is all there is to do,
we'll pick connecting spots of sky
for all our children, too.

ACKNOWLEDGMENTS

There are a little over 100 poems in this book. To get to 100 poems I thought were good enough, I had to write 1,000 poems. To write 1,000 poems, I had to start 10,000 poems, most of which sit unfinished in my phone, my laptop, my notebooks, or in deep caves in my brain. To start 10,000 poems required a dream. To see that dream realized in this book you hold in your hands, well, that required a whole lot from a whole lot of people who aren't me.

First, to the creative writing program at Sacramento State University, thank you for welcoming me. When I arrived to you, I was a lost soul who had just quit his career and decided to pursue a childhood dream of being a writer. I was terribly insecure and constantly wondered if I had just made the worst decision of my life. But by the time I graduated, you had filled me with enough knowledge and confidence that I knew this dream was not a childish pursuit. If I kept learning and kept writing, the dream was attainable . . . thank you.

To the Instagram poetry and writing community, thank you for your support. I started my account, @elisonwrites, at a dark time in my life and needed a place to put my thoughts and feelings. I didn't know my words would mean anything to anyone, but they did to you. Over the past few years, you have been the fuel to keep me writing . . . thank you.

To Michelle Halket, Beau Adler, Jessica Peirce, Molly Ringle, the team at Central Avenue, your belief in me and in my words has meant the world to me. It's rare to find a group of honest, smart, and passionate people just trying to bring more understanding and beauty to the world, and it has been a blessing to work with you . . . thank you.

To my brother, my friends, and my extended family, thank you for loving me. You showed up at random poetry readings, read terrible drafts of books I'd written, shared my work online, and told me when words I wrote meant something deeply to you. Hopefully each of you will now buy ten copies of this book for the people in your lives (just kidding, five is enough) . . . thank you.

To Mom and Dad, thank you for everything. You moved across the world to give your kids different opportunities, and that meant endless sacrifices once you got here. I like to think this book is in honor of the sacrifices you made. I also think the love between the two of you—more solid than the most solid thing on earth—triggered many of the poems in the Soulmates section of this book. For your support, sacrifice, and modeling of real love . . . thank you.

To my daughters, Emilia Fe and Finley Jax, you are only seven and three years old at the time of this writing, but thank you for opening and breaking and restructuring my heart in the most beautiful ways. I hope this book reinforces that no matter what direction your lives take you, there's always room for your dreams. You have my heart, but I don't expect you to be gentle with it. For being my reasons and for occasionally picking up your toys . . . thank you.

Lastly, to Patty, my wife, my love, thank you for being a much better partner than I deserve. There is some of us in this book, but much more of it remains unwritten. And that story, the one you and I have to tell together, is the best thing I will ever help write. For seeing me truly and still accepting me, thank you. But most of all, for just being you . . . thank you.

Elison Alcovendaz is a Filipino-American writer whose work has appeared in many acclaimed magazines and journals. His short prose was selected as a Best Small Fictions 2020 winner and has been nominated for Best of the Net. When he isn't writing, Elison collects books, shops at thrift stores, builds Lego, and chastises himself for indulging in these activities instead of writing. He lives in Sacramento, CA, with his wife and two daughters.

@elisonwrites